D0983465

MONSTERS

TROLLS

BY RACHEL LYNETTE

KIDHAVEN PRESS
A part of Gale, Cengage Learning

GALE
CENGAGE Learning

Detroit • New York • San Francisco • New Haven, Conn • Waterville, Maine • London

GALE
CENGAGE Learning

LIBRARY OF CONGRESS CATALOGING-IN-PUBLICATION DATA

Lynette, Rachel.
 Trolls / by Rachel Lynette.
   p. cm. -- (Monsters)
 Includes bibliographical references and index.
 ISBN 978-0-7377-4408-8 (hardcover)
 1. Trolls. I. Title.
 GR555.L96 2009
 398.21--dc22

                                                        2008051298

KidHaven Press
27500 Drake Rd.
Farmington Hills, MI 48331

ISBN-13: 978-0-7377-4408-8
ISBN-10: 0-7377-4408-1

Printed in the United States of America
1 2 3 4 5 6 7 13 12 11 10 09

CONTENTS

CHAPTER 1

TERRIBLE TROLLS

Once upon a time, two brothers got caught in the Hedal woods after dark. They had just made camp when they heard snuffling and snorting nearby. At first they thought it was a wild animal, but then they heard a loud voice say, "I smell the smell of Christian blood here!" [1] The younger brother was frightened, but the older brother knew what to do. He took the hatchet and hid in the bushes to watch.

There were three trolls, all as tall as the fir trees, but the boy noticed something strange; the front troll had a single eye. The other two each had an eye socket, but neither had an eye. Blindly, they followed the lead troll who had the eye. The boy realized that all three trolls shared the one eye. The boy snuck up behind the last troll and used his hatchet to chop at his ankle. The troll let out such a horrible shriek that the first troll jumped and dropped the eye. The boy scooped up the eye, leaving all three trolls blind.

The trolls were angry and threatened the boy, but he replied, "I'm not afraid of Trolls or threats. Now I have three eyes to myself, and you don't have any!" [2] The trolls begged him to give them back their eye. The boy finally agreed in exchange for two buckets of gold and silver. No one has seen the trolls in the Hedal woods since that day.

This story of *The Boys who Met the Trolls in the Hedal Woods* is an old one. It has been told for many years, and there are many different versions. Like many other troll stories, it involves a clever human outsmarting trolls.

STORIES FROM SCANDINAVIA

Stories about trolls were first told in Denmark, Sweden, Norway, and Finland. Together these four countries in Northern Europe are often called Scandinavia.

The origin of the word *troll* is unknown; however, several languages contain words that are somewhat like the word *troll.* In old Scandinavia, the word may have originally meant "magical,"

Stories about trolls originated in Scandinavia.

"**supernatural**," or "**perilous**." It also may have meant "someone who behaves violently." In Sweden, old laws refer to "trolleri" as a type of magic meant to hurt or destroy. Another possibility comes from the North Germanic language, in which the word *trolldom* means witchcraft and *trolla* means to perform magic tricks.

No one knows exactly where the idea of trolls came from. They may have originally been giants in **Norse** mythology. It also is possible that trolls first came from an ancient **pagan** ritual. In this ritual, people sat on grave mounds at night. They did this to honor the dead, or possibly to try to communicate with them. As Christianity gained popularity in the 10th and 11th centuries, people began to think of the old pagan religions as evil. Laws were passed to stop pagan rituals. The word *troll* appeared for the first time in some of these laws about grave sitters.

The Jætte Trolls

Most trolls tend to fall into one of two types. The first, and perhaps best known, are the jætte trolls. These are large, vicious trolls. They terrorize helpless villages and eat people whole. These trolls also may be known as giants, ogres, or cyclopes. They are usually covered in hair, may have tusks, and are always very strong. The troll that lives under the bridge in *The Three Billy Goats Gruff* is this kind of troll. In one version of the story the troll is

The tale of Three Billy Goats Gruff, *illustrated here, includes a jætte troll.*

described as, "big and ugly, and hairy, with eyes as round as saucers and teeth as sharp as knives." [3]

These trolls are **carnivorous**, and although the troll in *The Three Billy Goats Gruff* is hoping to make a goat his dinner, trolls generally prefer human meat. They believe that human meat is more tender and tasty than other meat.

Trolls are big and strong, but they are not very bright. Many a folk hero has taken advantage of this, outfoxing the trolls, then stealing their riches to gain wealth and fame for destroying the giant, hairy menace.

Jætte trolls usually live alone in caves, where they sleep during the day. At night they roam the forest, devouring whatever animals or humans they find. They may eat their victims on the spot or may bring them back to their cave to cook before eating.

THE VITTERFOLK TROLLS

The lesser-known trolls are called the vitterfolk trolls. Stories about vitterfolk trolls are more common in Southern Scandinavia. Vitterfolk trolls are much more intelligent than jætte trolls. They are clever and cunning. These trolls are about human size, or sometimes smaller. They also often behave like humans. They wear clothes, keep animals, and grow their food. Like their giant counterparts, they have a lot of hair. They also have tails, which they tend to keep hidden. In most cases, they are

Vitterfolk trolls are known for their long hair.

ugly; however, there are some stories about the women being very beautiful. Vitterfolk troll women are known for tromping around the forest in clothing that humans would consider to be much too fancy and elegant for the outdoors.

Vitterfolk trolls usually live in burrows, which they decorate richly. They usually live in groups or even in small villages. The vitterfolk often have large stashes of treasure. They usually hoard their gold and silver, but they will sometimes give some to people who please them.

Vitterfolk trolls are not always enemies to humans. They tend to treat humans in the same way that the humans treat them, returning acts of kindness. However, if they are provoked, their wrath may be worse than that of jætte trolls. They steal,

vandalize, and burn the property of those who anger them.

Vitterfolk trolls also are known for kidnapping babies, sometimes, leaving their own offspring in place of the human baby as a **changeling**. In the Middle Ages (500–1500 A.D.), **deformed** children were sometimes thought to be changelings. These children were often poorly cared for because their parents did not believe they were human. Some of these children were even put into the oven or left in the woods to starve. Parents sometimes treated these babies cruelly in hopes that that the changeling's troll mother would switch the babies again in order to save her own child.

TROLL MAGIC

In many tales, vitterfolk trolls can use magic. Troll magic can be used for many things. One of their most common feats of magic is the ability to become invisible. Trolls also are said to be able to fly on the wind. In addition, they can be **shapeshifters** and can disguise themselves as woodland animals, cats or dogs, or even as rocks or logs. Trolls especially enjoy changing into a rolling ball of yarn. When dealing with humans, they can charm them into doing whatever they ask. It also is thought that trolls may be able to erase human memories.

Because of their magic, vitterfolk trolls make great thieves. In many stories, humans will suddenly discover something is missing, but no one saw anyone in the house. Trolls can be mischievous. They may eat from people's plates when they are not looking or add something dreadful to a cooking pot and spoil the food.

Trolls sometimes take humans to be prisoners or slaves. Trolls usually choose children or people who are alone, such as a travelers or shepherds.

According to folklore, trolls sometimes take humans, preferably children, as prisoners.

These unlucky people are known as bergtagna, which means "taken to the mountain" or "spirited away." Bergtagna are sometimes freed after many years or even decades, but they usually had been driven insane by the trolls, or had their memories erased. It is possible that because people in the Middle Ages did not understand **mental illness**, they explained a mentally ill person's strange behavior by saying he or she was taken by trolls.

FIGHTING WITH TROLLS

Humans and trolls generally do not get along very well. In most cases, the troll, with its size, strength, and magic, has the advantage. In some cases, however, the human manages to get the best of the troll.

Trolls do have several weaknesses of which humans take advantage. All trolls hate light. They live in the dark most of the time, and light will blind them, and sometimes burn them. Sunlight is even worse for trolls; in some cases it will turn them to stone. In his famous book *The Hobbit*, J.R.R. Tolkien describes three trolls that were turned to stone by the sun. "And there they stand, to this day, all alone, unless the birds perch on them, for trolls, as you probably know, must be underground before dawn, or they go back to the stuff of the mountains they are made of, and never move again."[4]

Trolls also hate anything having to do with Christianity. The sound of church bells hurts them greatly. A cross also will ward them off, and even saying "Jesus" or "Christ" will make a troll cringe. There are stories of trolls who try to pre-

This illustration from The Hobbit *depicts three trolls eating around a fire as their prisoner, bottom left, tries to escape.*

vent churches from being built by sneaking onto the building site at night to destroy the work that was done during the day. They may even steal the church bell and take it far away. In some legends, trolls also are afraid of steel.

Most people today do not believe in trolls. However, in the Middle Ages, people believed in many supernatural creatures, such as demons and witches. To them, trolls were real. Stories about the cruelty of trolls could be used to make children obey for fear of being left in the woods for the trolls. Stories of humans getting the best of trolls were not only amusing, but also helped to ward off fear of the unknown.

CHAPTER 2

TROLL TALES

Trolls have appeared in stories and lore the world over, from their Scandinavian roots to modern times. Some of the stories are gruesome and horrific, while others are uplifting with happy endings.

TROLLS IN THE MIDDLE AGES

In medieval times, many troll stories were short tales of things that were believed to have actually happened. It could be a story of a traveler who was eaten by trolls or a village that was overrun by them. Stories of swapping human babies for changelings, or troll babies, also were common.

In one changeling story, a mother troll trades her own troll baby for that of a human baby boy. The human parents soon realize that the child is not their own baby, but a troll. The father encourages the mother to leave the baby troll in the woods to die, but she refuses, saying the troll baby, though ugly, is innocent. The townspeople also try to convince the mother to be unkind to the child, saying that if she beats the baby with a heavy stick, the troll mother will return the human baby. The mother again refuses to hurt the troll baby. She cares for the baby for several years, all the while, missing her own baby terribly. The townspeople treat her cruelly for caring for a troll. Her husband finally throws the troll child into a fire, and the mother risks her own life to save him.

After the fire, the husband leaves his wife saying that he will not live with a troll. While walking in the woods he meets his own son. The son tells him that because his mother treated the troll baby kindly, the troll mother treated him with kindness. However, when the father treated the troll child cruelly, his own son was treated to the same punishments. He too, would have perished in a fire had not his own mother saved the troll baby. It was his mother's willingness to risk her own life for the troll child that finally broke the troll's power over the human boy, so he could return home. Mother and child are reunited, all because of the mother's kindness to the troll changeling.

 Trolls

Fairy Tale Trolls

Like many folktales, most troll stories were passed down from person to person. Some well-known fairy tales may have had their beginnings in Scandinavian troll lore. The tale of Rumpelstiltskin has a great deal in common with a folktale from Den-

The story of Rumpelstiltskin (right) may have gotten its origins from a Danish folktale involving a troll named Fin.

mark about a troll named Fin. Although there is no baby or spinning straw into gold in this story, the hero of the story does have to guess the troll's name. If he fails to do so, the troll will take his heart and his eyes. Just as in the story of Rumpelstiltskin, the troll's name is overheard in the woods and the hero guesses correctly.

In the mid-1800s, two Norwegian writers named Peter Asbjærnsen and Jærgen Moe put many of the folk stories that had been passed from person to person into a book. Their collection of Norwegian fairy tales was first published in 1845 and includes several stories about trolls, including the well-known *Three Billy Goats Gruff* and *The Boys who Met the Trolls in the Hedal Woods.*

Another collection of troll tales is *Bland Tomtar och Troll,* which translates to "Among Gnomes and Trolls." This annual Swedish magazine began in 1907 and is still published today.

"The Ash Lad who Had an Eating Match with the Troll"

One of the stories of Asbjærnsen and Moe is that of "The Ash Lad who Had an Eating Match with the Troll. " According to the story, there once was an old and ailing farmer who had three sons. He owned a plot of land with woods on it, but he also had debts to pay off, so he asked his sons to cut some wood to sell. The eldest son was just starting to cut down a spruce tree when a troll came lum-

"IF YOU DON'T BE QUIET," SHOUTED THE LAD TO THE TROLL, "I'LL SQUEEZE YOU
JUST AS I SQUEEZE THE WATER OUT OF THIS STONE"

*In a Norwegian folktale, Askeladen, or Ash Lad,
fools a troll into thinking he is so powerful that he
can squeeze water from a rock. In reality, the Ash
Lad was squeezing whey from a block of cheese.*

bering into view and thundered, "If you're chopping in my forest, I'm going to kill you!" [5]

Troll Tales  21

The boy dropped his ax and ran as fast as he could to the house and gasped out the story to his father. The father got angry at him, saying that the trolls never scared him when he was young. The second-eldest son tried the next day, but the same thing happened to him, and the father scolded the panting youth, reminding him that he had never been afraid of trolls when he was young.

The youngest son, who was called the Ash Lad, or Askeladen, said he would try. The two older sons were skeptical, because of his youth and lack of strength. His mother was making cheese, and even though it was not yet done, he took some anyway. When he got to the forest, the troll came out and boomed out, "If you're chopping in my forest, I'm going to kill you!"[6]

The boy was prepared, and took the half-made cheese from his knapsack and squeezed the **whey** out of it, saying, "If you don't hold your tongue, I'll squeeze you the way I'm squeezing the water out of this white stone!"[7] The troll was afraid and offered to help the Ash Lad chop the wood if he would spare his life. The troll was a good lumberjack, and they got a lot of wood. They went back to the troll's cave because it was closer than the house. At the cave, the troll asked the boy to go for water while he lit a fire to make porridge. The buckets for water were so big that the Ash Lad could not even move them, so he bluffed again. "It's not worth taking along these thimbles. I'm going after the whole well, I am!"[8]

The troll realized that he needed his well and said that he would get the water while the Ash Lad lit the fire. When the troll came back with the water, they boiled the porridge in an enormous pot. Then the Ash Lad had one last idea. He asked the troll if he would like to have an eating contest, and the troll readily accepted, knowing he could win. They sat down with the giant pot of porridge. The Ash Lad had hidden his knapsack and had tied it on his stomach under his shirt. Then, while he and the troll were eating the porridge, he secretly started slipping porridge into the pouch instead of his mouth. When the knapsack was full, the Ash Lad took out his knife and cut a hole in it and the porridge came spilling out. The troll was shocked, but said nothing. Then the troll put down his spoon and said, "Nay! Now I can't manage any more!"[9]

The boy responded, "I'm barely half full yet. Do as I did and cut a hole in your stomach, then you can eat as much as you wish!"[10] The troll cut open his own stomach, and soon died. Then the Ash Lad searched deeper into the troll's cave and found the troll's hoard of gold and silver. He took it home and with it he was able to pay off his family's debts.

Troll Art

Many artists have drawn trolls. Theodor Kittelsen and John Bauer are two of the more well-known troll artists. Kittelsen was born in Norway and

loved the natural scenery of his country. In his drawings the trolls are sometimes a part of the scenery, blending in with rocks and trees. Many of Kittelsen's best-known troll pictures can be found in later editions of *Asbjœrnsen and Moe's Collection of Norwegian Fairy Tales*.

John Bauer created illustrations for eight volumes of *Bland Tomtar och Troll*. One way that Bauer's trolls are different from those of other artists is the way he draws their eyes. Bauer's trolls have expressive eyes that often make them look kind, curious, or playful.

TROLL POEMS

Trolls also have found their way into poetry. Often these poems are silly or scary. "Monday's Troll," by children's poet Jack Prelutsky, is a silly one. It describes different trolls for each day of the week.

An older poem by the Swedish poet Gustaf Fræding, takes a different approach. This poem is narrated by the troll himself who is thinking of making a beautiful young princess his dinner:

> And into a sack I'll get her,
> And take her home with me straight,
> And then at Yule I will eat her
> Served up on a fine gold plate.[11]

In the end, the troll decided not to eat the princess because, instead of running from him in fright as other people did, she was kind to him.

Children's poet Jack Prelutsky, author of "Monday's Troll."

TROLL TALES TODAY

Trolls do not just show up in fairy tales of old; they also stomp their way through several modern fantasy books. One of the most famous is *The Hobbit* by J.R.R. Tolkien, which was first published in 1937. In this book, the small hobbit Bilbo, encounters three trolls as they are eating mutton around a fire. Although he has never seen a troll before, Bilbo knows they are trolls, "from the great heavy faces of them, and their size, and the shape of their

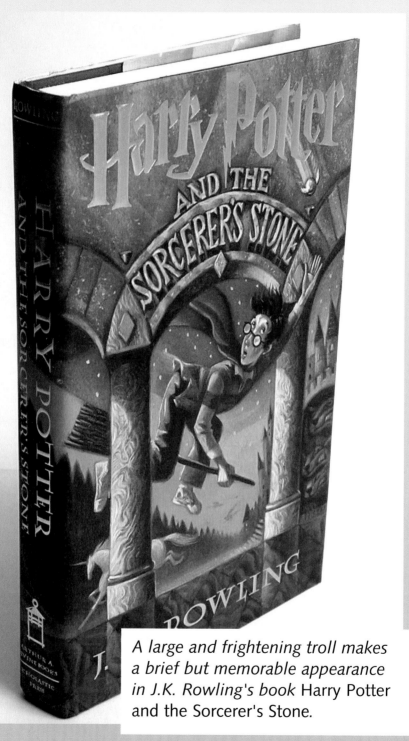

A large and frightening troll makes a brief but memorable appearance in J.K. Rowling's book Harry Potter and the Sorcerer's Stone.

legs, not to mention their language, which was not drawing-room fashion, at all, at all."[12] Bilbo, along with his dwarf friends, are nearly eaten by the trolls. They are saved by the wizard Gandalf, who tricks the trolls into staying above ground when the sun comes up.

Unlike Tolkien's trolls, the moomin trolls created in a series of books by Finnish author Tove Jansson are cute, kind, and playful. They live in the woods of Finland, where they get into all kinds of adventures. These whimsical stories, which were first published in the 1940s and 1950s are still popular with children today.

Another author whose trolls are more playful than scary is Jan Brett. In the beautifully illustrated picture book, *Trouble with Trolls* (1992), a clever girl named Treva tricks a pack of trolls out of stealing her dog.

Children today are most familiar with the troll that Harry and Ron fight in *Harry Potter and the Sorcerer's Stone* (1997) by J.K. Rowling. Rowling describes the troll:

> It was a horrible site. Twelve feet tall, its
> skin was a dull granite gray, its great lumpy
> body like a boulder with its small bald head
> perched on top like a coconut. It had short
> legs thick as tree trunks with flat, horny feet.
> The smell coming from it was incredible.
> It was holding a huge wooden club, which

dragged along the floor because its arms were so long.[13]

Author Katherine Langrish wrote her three troll books, *Troll Fell* (2004), *Troll Mill* (2006), and *Troll Blood* (2008), in the style of a Scandinavian fairy tale. The books are filled with mystical creatures, including many terrifying trolls. Trolls also appear in Eoin Colfer's Artemis Fowl books and in the Spiderwick Chronicles by Holly Black. Although each author describes his or her trolls a little differently, all were inspired by the trolls from Scandinavia.

Chapter 3

Trolls Among Us

It is not just people in Scandinavia who are fascinated by trolls. Trolls can be found throughout Europe and the United States in the movies, on TV, and in video games. Some people even collect trolls.

In the Movies and on TV

Trolls occasionally show up as minor characters in the movies. There was a troll in both *Harry Potter and the Sorcerer's Stone* and *The Lord of the Rings: The Fellowship of the Ring*. In both movies, the heroes successfully fight a large, vicious, and stupid troll.

In 1986 a troll named Torok got a starring role. The movie *Troll* was about an ancient troll who

THE
LORD OF RINGS
THE FELLOWSHIP OF THE RING

A troll was featured in the highly acclaimed 2001 movie The Lord of the Rings: The Fellowship of the Ring.

uses a magic ring to try and turn the modern world into the ancient one he once lived in. The movie features a dark-haired boy named Harry Potter Jr. who discovers he can do magic. J.K. Rowling has been accused of **plagiarizing** the character for her own books. Rowling says that there is no relation between her Harry Potter and the one in *Troll*, although she does admit that she may have seen *Troll* as a child. There are plans to remake *Troll* in 2009. In the new version, the actor who played Harry Potter Jr. in the 1986 film will take on the role of Torok.

Troll 2 was made in 1990, but was not related at all to the 1986 movie. In fact, the movie featured no trolls at all. The movie did not do well at the box office and was even featured in a 2004 **documentary** called *The 50 Worst Movies Ever Made*. Over the years, however, the movie has developed a loyal cult following through video and DVD.

Trolls also have appeared in several TV shows. In *The Boy Who Loved Trolls*, a 1984 made-for-TV movie, a boy risks everything to save a troll he finds under a bridge. Other shows that have featured trolls include the *Power Rangers, Bewitched,* and *Buffy the Vampire Slayer*. In 2005 Nickelodeon produced an animated show called *Kung Fu Spy Troll,* but it never aired.

TECHNOLOGY TROLLS

Believe it or not, there are trolls all over the Internet, but not the big and hairy kind. The term *troll* is used to describe a person who posts messages in **forums** and discussion boards that are meant to make people angry. Instead of participating in the ongoing discussion, these people write insulting and offensive messages. Often they intentionally use poor spelling or grammar, many exclamation points, and inappropriate language. Although trolls sometimes succeed in making people angry, most people simply ignore them. Often, their messages are deleted, and they are blocked from posting again.

The more traditional fantasy trolls also can be found in many video and computer games, almost

A computer screen shows a scene from the online video game World of Warcraft, *one of the world's most popular video games.*

always as enemies. In most cases, they are obstacles the main character must overcome. One of the first examples of this was in the arcade classic game *Joust*, in which a lava troll attempts to pull the jousters into the lava. Only the troll's hand and arm are visible, however, and it is not widely known that it is a troll. Other more current games that feature trolls include *Guild Wars*, *Fable II*, and *Final Fantasy XI*.

In at least one video game a troll is a playable character. In the worldwide, multiplayer role-playing game *World of Warcraft*, a player can choose to be a troll. Trolls in this game are tall and slender with blue or green skin. As a troll, the player can then interact with thousands of other fantasy characters.

COLLECTING TROLLS

Many people collect troll figurines or dolls. These may be handmade and sold at street fairs, crafts fairs, and gift shops as well as online. Often these are whimsical creatures with expressive faces. There also are collectible troll figures from the *Lord of the Rings* movies.

However, the most popular collectable trolls are the small vinyl ones made by Russ® and other novelty companies. These trolls have big eyes, giant smiles, and wild, colorful hair. The original trolls were made by Danish woodcutter Thomas Dam in the 1950s. The first trolls were carved from wood and

The smiling, little trolls with colorful hair were popular collectibles in the 1960s and 1990s.

had sheep's wool hair and glass eyes. Later, they were made from soft rubber and finally vinyl. They soon became known as "Dam Dolls" or "Dam Things." These are still the most valuable trolls today. Some are worth hundreds, even thousands of dollars. The popularity of these trolls inspired many other toy companies to make their own, less-expensive versions.

Imitation trolls, sometimes called Wishkin Trolls, Treasure Trolls, Gonks, or Norfins, spread throughout Europe and North America. Thousands of different trolls have been made. Although most look happy, playful, or mischievous, there also are mean, angry, and crafty trolls. Most of these trolls come with clothing. This can be traditional troll garb, or they may be dressed in modern-day wear. A troll may be dressed as a teacher, a firefighter, or a rock star. There are trolls that represent almost any career or hobby. Trolls in holiday clothing

have been particularly popular as they make fun gifts. These troll dolls were at the peak of their popularity from 1963 through 1965, when their sales were second only to Barbie™. The trolls were thought to bring good luck and most people had at least one. The trend died down in the 1970s and 1980s. Trolls made a comeback in the 1990s as adults became **nostalgic** for things from their younger days. Today, many people still collect trolls. Serious collectors own thousands of them.

Troll collector, Jennifer Miller, has turned the front of her New York apartment into a troll museum. Miller has a story for every troll in her museum. The collection itself is not one of the more valuable ones; however, it means a great deal to Miller who says, "The amount of smiles these trolls have mustered out of me on even the most dismal afternoons, is worth more than could be expressed in terms of capital [money]. They are my muse, inspiring me, when all I see is darkness and oppression."[14]

Troll Town

It is not just collectors who love trolls. The town of Mount Horeb in Wisconsin is known as Troll Town because of its many statues and images of trolls. Many of the houses in the area have troll statues on their front lawns. There are trolls carved into tree trunks along the "Trollway," where visitors are

The Fremont Troll is a giant troll sculpture lurking under the Aurora Bridge in the Fremont district of Seattle, Washington.

encouraged to take a "Troll Stroll." There are even signs that say "Troll X-ing" (or Troll Crossing). Most tourists are charmed by the many trolls, but visitor Lynn Van Hoose found them a little frightening, "I was slightly scared by the amount of trolls in the city. They are everywhere! Even the street signs have little trolls on them. A local dentist's sign has a troll holding a toothbrush."[15]

Another place to find a famous troll is under the Aurora Bridge in Seattle, Washington. The troll is called the Fremont Troll because it is located in the Fremont district of Seattle. The street on which the troll resides was renamed Troll Avenue in its honor. Created by four artists in 1990, this troll is made of reinforced concrete. It is nearly 20 feet (6m) tall, and weighs more than 2 tons (1814Kg). The troll appears to crush a real Volkswagon Beetle in one hand, as though he has just swiped it off the bridge above. One of the car's hubcaps was used to make one of the troll's two eyes. Unlike most pieces of art, people are encouraged to climb on the troll. The troll is the site of an annual Halloween party known as "Trollaween." The Fremont Troll also can be seen in the movie *10 Things I Hate About You.*

TROLLS FOREVER

From ancient Scandinavian times to today, trolls have captured people's imaginations. Whether they are cute and fuzzy or mean and ugly, the trolls of

fantasy and legend have been scaring and entertaining us for years. Although most people do not believe in trolls today, perhaps they live on. As author Michael Berenstain says in *The Troll Book*,

> Trolls are now a hidden race, unseen and unknown, their very existence doubted by some. Only in the forgotten corners of the wild do they still survive–places where humankind has never set foot and, perhaps never will.[16]

Notes

Chapter 1: Terrible Trolls

1. Peter Christen Asbjærnsen and Jærgen Moe, *Norwegian Folktales*, New York: Pantheon Books, 1982, p. 10.
2. Asbjærnsen and Moe, *Norwegian Folktales*, p. 10.
3. Joanne Asala, *Norwegian Troll Tales*, Iowa City, IA: Penfield, 2005, p. 101.
4. J.R.R. Tolkien, *The Hobbit*, New York: Ballantine, 1979, pp. 51–52.

Chapter 2: Troll Tales

5. Asbjærnsen and Moe, *Norwegian Folktales*, p. 81.
6. Asbjærnsen and Moe, *Norwegian Folktales*, p. 83.
7. Asbjærnsen and Moe, *Norwegian Folktales*, p. 83.
8. Asbjærnsen and Moe, *Norwegian Folktales*, p. 83.
9. Asbjærnsen and Moe, *Norwegian Folktales*, p. 83.
10. Asbjærnsen and Moe, *Norwegian Folktales*, p. 83.
11. Gustaf Fræding, "The Old Mountain Troll," Trollmoon, http://users.skynet.be/fa023784/trollmoon/TrollWriters/trollwriters.html.
12. Tolkien, *The Hobbit*, pp. 51–52.
13. J.K. Rowling, *Harry Potter and the Sorcerer's Stone*, New York: Scholastic, 1997, p. 174.

14. Jennifer Miller, "Reverend Jen's Lower East Side Troll Museum," press release, www.society ofcontrol.com/coal/rev_troll.htm.

15. Lynn Van Hoose, "Mount Horeb, Wisconsin: Troll Infested Town," RoadsideAmerica.com, May 31, 2007, www.roadsideamerica.com/ tip/1456.

16. Michael Berenstain, *The Troll Book*, New York: Random House, 1980.

GLOSSARY

carnivorous: Feeding on the flesh of animals.

changeling: A nonhuman child that has been secretly switched with a human one by fairies or trolls.

deformed: Abnormally formed or misshapen.

documentary: A movie or TV show that provides factual information.

forums: Internet discussion groups.

mental illness: Any disease of the mind that causes abnormal behavior.

Norse: Relating to ancient Scandinavia.

nostalgic: A longing for things from the past.

pagan: Ancient religions that worship many gods.

perilous: Full of danger.

plagiarizing: Using another person's ideas or work and claiming it as one's own.

shape-shifters: Creatures that are able to change their appearance so they look like something else.

supernatural: Something that cannot be explained by science.

vandalize: To deliberately destroy or damage property.

whey: The watery part of milk that separates from the solid part when making cheese.

FOR FURTHER EXPLORATION

BOOKS

Joanne Asala, *Norwegian Troll Tales*, Iowa City, IA: Penfield, 2005. This collection of troll stories includes works from Asbjærnsen and Moe as well as the artwork of Theodor Kittelsen.

Ingri and Edgar Parin D'Aurlaire, *D'Aulaires' Book of Trolls*, New York: New York Review Children's Collection, 2006. This illustrated book contains several stories of trolls from Scandinavia.

Tove Jansson, *Moomin: The Complete Tove Jansson Comic Strip—Book 1. Montreal: Drawn and Quarterly, 2006.* The first of five books, this is a collection of comics that were created during the period that Jansson was writing her Moomin chapter books and were published in London's *Evening News*.

Katherine Langrish, *Troll Fell*, New York: Harper-Collins, 2005. This is the first in the Trolls trilogy in which young Peer encounters many mythical characters, including some mischievous trolls.

Pat Peterson, *Collector's Guide to Trolls: Identification*

and Values, Paducah, KY: Collector Books, 1995. This book features more than one thousand color pictures of troll dolls as well as information about their values.

J.R.R. Tolkien, *The Hobbit, 70th Anniversary Edition,* New York: Houghton Mifflin, 2007. This seventieth anniversary edition of the classic book by Tolkien includes an introduction by his son, Christopher Tolkien. Look for trolls in the chapter titled "Roast Mutton."

J.K. Rowling, *Harry Potter and the Sorcerer's Stone,* New York: Scholastic, 1997. Harry and his friends fight a troll at Hogwarts in this first Harry Potter book.

WEB SITES

Family Fun (http://familyfun.go.com/arts-and-crafts/cutpaste/feature/famf39kidcot/famf39 kidcot4.html). This Web page offers instructions for a craft project on how to make trolls out of corks.

Legends of the Trolls (http://library. thinkquest.org/12924/). This Web page offers information about Norwegian culture, trolls, troll stories, and an interactive troll quiz.

INDEX

Picture Credits

ABOUT THE AUTHOR

Rachel Lynette has never seen a real troll, though she does own a troll doll with purple hair. Lynette would like to thank her son, David, for his help with this book. Lynette has written more than 40 books for children as well as resource materials for teachers. She lives in the Seattle, Washington, area in the Songaia Cohousing Community with her two delightful children, David and Lucy, and a cat named Cosette. When she is not teaching or writing, Lynette enjoys spending time with her family and friends, traveling, reading, drawing, crocheting colorful hats, and inline skating.